How to Create Fun and Effective Developmental Swim Practices

Jeffrey Napolski

Published by Jeffrey Napolski, 2019.

HOW TO CREATE FUN AND EFFECTIVE DEVELOPMENTAL SWIM PRACTICES

First edition. July 25, 2019.

Written by Jeffrey Napolski.

Introduction - Who are you and why do I care?

THE FIRST TIME I COACHED a swim team I had no idea what I was doing. Not a clue. I was 20, still in college, and the pool I worked at over the summer asked me to start a swim team. This was the summer of 2000 and I had been working at my pool for 5 summers. Looking back I think it was because I was a responsible and effective swim instructor. It helped that I had been on the swim team in high school, but I had only been on the JV team. At that point I had only about 6 months experience in competitive swimming total; 3 months each year. I never swam on club teams. I never went to day long meets, and the only practices I ever went to were immediately after school with Freshman and Sophomores when I was a Junior and Senior. But there I was, coaching a summer league outdoor pool team, and we had 40 kids registered to show up for practice Monday - Thursday at 6am.

I'm ashamed now to say I showed up late pretty often after being out the night before with my friends. Despite the occasional late arrival the kids and parents loved the experience, they loved me working with their kids and I loved it too. I would run that summer league team for the next three summers and it grew every year. It still exists, and is over 200 strong each summer.

Ultimately, I think it was that experience that helped me get a job as an assistant swim coach with a local USA Swimming club team, and in the first year I was helping to coach kids that were winning Illinois Age Group championship races. Eventually I took over the mid level groups on the swim team, and then became the Head Developmental Coach where I am the lead for 100 swimmers across three groups from beginners to starting to be competitive. I've been coaching the developmental program for 5 years. There is no practice requirement, we have practice four days a week, and we're at a 4 lane 20 yard pool.

How is this possible?

Well, that is what we're going to talk about. If you're familiar with Swimming Ideas, I'm all about finding out what works, trying something new, and seeing if it has success and fits.

Most of all I coach and teach swimming lessons with this one mindset: are the students "reaching" and learning effectively?

This book is going to walk you through how we structure our practices, what the words, scripts, and ways we speak to translate language into swimming action. You will learn how we go from barely being able to swim to competing in regional swim meets in one of the fastest states in the nation.

We're going to look at the pieces that make up a fun and effective swim team practice across all beginning levels.

We'll look at how we can promote deliberate practice to aim effort at very specific techniques.

This book will also look at how we can teach high quality swimming in a safe and encouraging environment.

When I coach I'm looking for perfection; and I get close to it while still having fun. I want perfection with an opportunity to fail and make another attempt.

Yes, the ultimate goal is excellence and we can create a culture where great swimming is expected, but to get there we encourage, expect, and allow for spectacular failure.

This book is about how you can have fun and effective swim practices.

You can get some really good information as well from our podcast. Check out episode number 057: An Interview with Meighan Julbert, MS. We talk about being comfortable in the uncomfortable, why it is okay to fail, and the number one rule she gives her coach clients.

Effectiveness

———

Finding Deliberate Practice

I REMEMBER THE FIRST time I started coaching the developmental groups that I run now. I was salty and upset. Not because I thought it was beneath me but because I finally saw what our part time developmental coaches were doing. It wasn't because we didn't have quality coaches, or that they didn't know what to do. They just weren't great at it; they were part time, showing up with no plan on what to do, and had little to no training on how to be an effective coach. Before I took over I was their assistant coach so I could learn what to do.

It was excruciatingly boring. So boring that I would have to turn away from the pool to hide my annoyance, to cover my ire at the waste of time. Looking back I should have spoken up, I should have said something to correct their behavior; but I was intruding on their group.

Coaches are territorial.

Have you ever felt like your swim group is your castle and you are their king or queen? Like you know all the kids, you have a general plan for what you want them to do, and you write the practices and you are the speaker? Your group is your kingdom and the livelihood of your swimmers is your responsibility.

The reason I turned my face away from these mediocre developmental coaches when I started as their assistant was because they spoke too much. They loved hearing their own voices.

They pontificated, they speechified, they gabbed with the excessive effluence that was lost on their 5-9 year old audience. I began counting lengths and engagement one day because I was so offended by what this one coach was doing. In the course of a 45 minute practice for the beginning group, what was Developmental 1, they did 4 lengths. 4x 25's in 45 minutes. Do you know what they did the rest of the time? It wasn't skill work. It wasn't deliberate practice where they were given a task to complete. Nope. You know what they did? They sat at the side and listened to the coach talk about how to do freestyle perfectly. The coach blathered for long minutes as he tossed a ball up and down; barely paying attention to the kids or even following a coherent train of thought. I remember thinking "when is he going to get to the point? When is he going to let them *do* something?"

Do you think that your 6 year old or 8 year old would listen to you speak for 30 minutes about swimming front crawl and then do it perfectly on their first try? Of course not! They obviously swam the whole way as fast as they could and then bounced around splashing and doing flips because they were bored out of their minds and not learning anything! Things would have to change.Wasted time should not be tolerated when we could be using it productively.

My background is in swimming lessons. I've taught swim lessons since I was 16, and am now 39. That is almost 20 years of teaching (I say almost because I took a few years off in between). When I started coaching the USA Swimming team I felt like it was big time, it was for real, and not just side breathing. There was technique, there were even differing arguments for how to swim freestyle or other strokes best. But there I was with ineffective coaches watching them talk for over half the practice while their swimmers stood in the deep end and struggled to listen.

In the last five years I've failed repeatedly at providing fun and effective swim practices. I'm certain that I've done just as terrible, ineffective, and had resounding failures. There were times I lost my temper and screamed a a kid for not doing what I wanted. I've wasted time at practice because I was bored. I've sat on the bench and watched swimmers do mindless laps because I was feeling lazy. I've talked too long and go lost in flowery descriptions while having the swimmers get bored.

But in the last 5 years I've made efforts to improve. I've evaluated my performance. I've thought about how to improve and documented it on swimminglessonsideas.com. I've asked for help from my assistant coaches. I've asked for feedback and what we can do better. Looking back I'm going to focus on what went well.

I leaned on what I knew. I knew swim lessons. I shoehorned swim lesson tactics into our Developmental program. It was a natural fit because in swim lessons we maximize our time on task. One of the biggest metrics for success is "how often is the swimmer in the lesson participating?"

Think about a swim lesson or a swim practice. Are the people in the water stationary? Do you immediately think of them listening while standing around or did you picture them moving in the water?

My guess is you initially thought of a pool or water, then people moving around in it. Swimmers swim. Funny! We're teaching them to swim, we need to talk, we need to instruct and give feedback, but how can we do it in such a way that our swimmers are able to move with deliberate direction to get better.

The structure I have refined over the last six years working exclusively with the first three levels of our swim team and over half of our participants is outlined here. We have fun and effective swim practices that maximize deliberate practice to get results. At this point I want you to know it hasn't all been roses and pizza parties, cheeseburgers and french fries without high cholesterol. This book is the cumulation of six years of trial and error.

In those first few years I blundered through the systems we're going to review in this book. They have been tested with a constant look at the effectiveness of my planning. I have been blessed with extremely effective assistant coaches through the years that I've bounced ideas off of, asked for their input, and who had the freedom to tell me that something wasn't working. Some times I resisted their opinions, because "what would they know, they are only working two nights a week." But there are times when a critical outside eye sees what you're blind to, and my assistant coaches did that for me.

Lauren, Neil, Skye, Megan, Chloe, Joey, Nick, Elliot, TaeLee, and Jane. You've all helped me get to a point where I'm confident about sharing the patterns and routines you helped create through our failures and successes. Thank you.

Along with help from my assistant coaches I've always asked myself after every practice, "what could I have done better?" and "how can we do it better next time?" If you follow my Developmental Swim Practices, a subscription you can buy online, you'll notice that I do the same game three or four times in a row with minor adjustments. This is the living, breathing example of creating effective practices. You come up with a great idea, test it out, adjust what doesn't work, attempt it again with those changes, and refine it until you have a fun, effective, productive game that improves your swimmer's skills.

At the heart, this is what we're aiming at for you as a coach, and your swimmers. How do you find deliberate practice as a coach getting better at writing practices, and for your swimmers?

I think James Clear is the best at defining "deliberate practice." Check out his explanation of it here: https://jamesclear.com/deliberate-practice-theory.[1] Essentially, it is a special type of "practice" that is specific, deliberate, and systematic characterized by focused attention to improvement. I want you, and your swimmers to think, "I am doing this specifically to improve my stroke [or coaching] in this exact way."

My number one goal during swim practices is to provide as many opportunities for "deliberate practice" as possible. The

1. http://jamesclear.com/deliberate-practice-theory

framework, and the structure of our practices are refined into chunks designed to exploit attentive improvement and recharge with fun games and activities. A significant portion of this book is about "3x SL + [something]" which is the heart of deliberate practice. Additionally we do shorter 25's and 50's with specific attention to working on core learned skills in our small groups. As you read look for the framework and how you can adapt it to your program, then remember this basic format: activity, activity, game/challenge.

What do you mean by "fun" and "effective?"

––––––

Fun and effective swim games, and fun and effective swim practices. Great titles and headlines, but what exactly does it mean to have fun swim practices and how do you define effective? Great questions!

By "fun" we mean interesting and stimulating activities. I mean, fun is fun, but as a swim coach designing activities for children, I think, how can we get them to learn and do things in a fun way. Fun is sometimes a challenge, or a difficult hurdle that is overcome. I think about putting roadblocks in front of the kids and then give them the tools to overcome those bumps. Sometimes they are bigger mountains than others, and the effort that it takes to succeed over those speed-bumps provides satisfaction and fun. I also think that to keep things fun challenges have to be slightly different, or outside of the norm so it is interesting enough to pay attention to. The same stale boring routines can deaden your effort and lead to excessive plateaus.

By fun, I think challenging and engaging. A good measure of this is how interested are the kids in their daily practice behavior. Are they bored? Are they "going through the motions?"

Fun is a state of mind and approach; are the participants interacting with the coaches and responding to feedback while motivated to succeed at the tasks given? Not everything we do is fun, but are we injecting enough opportunities to stimulate their young minds to create an interesting and intriguing series of activities; or fun?

By "effective," I mean "are you getting results." Do the things you do with your swimmers make them better at competitive swimming in some fashion? Effective is the term I use to gauge whether or not the activity we come up with both serves a purpose and gives the swimmer some sort of additional skill. Effective skill learning can be anything from learning to move your body in the water to executing a precise flip turn.

Together each activity has to meet both requirements: fun and effective. These two are the basic metrics I use for a successful swimming activity, and a productive and results driven exciting practice. So if you want to learn how to make every practice interesting and fun but still get results read on!

What Is Routine And Why You Should Care

———

" We are what we repeatedly do. Excellence then, is not an act, but a habit." - Aristotle

From Oxford Dictionary service through Bing.com:

rou·tine

[rooˉ tēn]

1. a sequence of actions regularly followed; a fixed program:

"I settled down into a routine of work and sleep" ·

"as a matter of routine a report will be sent to the director"

ORIGIN

late 17th cent. (denoting a regular course or procedure): from French, from route 'road'

Routine is a way to establish habit, and to repeatedly do things well at your practices. I guess you could take this one maxim as the foundation for this whole book. If you listen to the Swimming Ideas Podcast we've been exploring deliberate practice and finding mastery. I've discovered that much of what we were already doing at developmental practices and swim lessons were expressing these ideas of dedicated learning and deliberate practice. My goal with this book was to drive down into what makes our practices so effective and fun.

Routine is the framework that allows us to do interesting and fun activities. When I get frustrated by boring practices with beginners it is because they don't know all the shorthand, they're not familiar yet with the routines I have built up in the more experienced groups. But recognizing those frustrations and discovering why they irritate us lead to this book and a close examination of our own program. It provided this question: "how do you get those beginners into your routine?" and "how do you establish your routine so we can then do those fun interesting activities with ease?"

Routine

———

The first step to a fun and effective swim practice is establishing your routines. When I say "routines" I mean the framework of your practices. In general you should give your swimmers a clear expectation of what they'll do at practice. That can mean doing a similarly formatted warm-up every day, or it could mean always starting every activity at a specific place in the pool. Once you establish a set standard of organization you can start layering small changes and differences to make your activities fun and effective.

After our warm-up we usually split up into two groups. I send half of the kids with an assistant coach to the other end of the lane/pool, and I take the half that remains at our start end. We do two different activities using 1/2 the pool. When the kids hear, "lanes one and two go to the deep end with Coach Lauren," they know immediately that they're going to be doing some sort of high skill practice with a specific focus. In the same way they know when I say, "get your fins," they're going to be doing something with the fins on their feet. We do this often enough that the swimmers move quickly into two groups and gather around the coaches for instructions. It seems seamless and quick. They are familiar with the routine yet are interested because the activities within the framework are so variable.

Provide some expected frameworks that you can easily flow through and in during each practice. Think of your routine as the letters to your alphabet, or the acronyms to your long complicated phrases. At our practices and swim lessons our routines center around 3 x streamline + [something] and circle swimming. You can find extensive information on the "rotation method" for swim lessons and short distance skill work at the end of this book or on my website, https://swimminglessonsideas.com

Whatever you chose for your routines, make sure that it is a simple scaffolding to hold all the different activities that you want to do. Find a rhythm and a flow that works for you and your swimmers can easily jump into once they know the basics.

Take a moment to think about what you do at the beginning of every season. How do you structure your first practice of the season in September? Most age group club teams have August off after championships. Their biggest tryouts and influx of new kids are in the fall that following September. It certainly is that way with our team. Take a brief moment to think about the plan you have in place, or what steps you take to get those new swimmers into your program.

Every fall in September I have a large group of new kids. Children that have never been on a swim team before. We average about 30 - 40 kids that are brand new to swimming on a competitive team and have never done a large group practice ranging in ages from 5 to 12. On any given day they can show up for their 45 minute practice in a tiny four lane 20 yard pool. Do you know why the first few weeks are so chaotic?

There are multiple reasons to be sure. There is the confusion of not knowing what the coach is saying, there is the distraction of a large group, the new setting, the strange tall man speaking loud, the women walking around smiling at people and asking their names. It can be a lot to take in. We also have a lot of people that don't know where to go in the water. They don't know what a 100 IM is, or even what butterfly kick means, or how to do breaststroke kick. They are true beginners. The first group on our swim team may also have people that have been in that group before that know some of the routines, but not everything, or maybe they struggle with particular skills keeping them in the introductory group. So you have some kids that all the introduction is a review and boring, and a whole host of others that are overwhelmed by the new information.

But at the heart of it all the lack of routine creates the most disruption.

Here are some basic words and phrases we use to establish standard behavior:

- Set up your lane: one person stands in the lane in the right corner (looking down the lane). Everyone else in the lane lines up from the left corner along the lane line or wall. If you're standing behind the lane it would look like an "L" shape.

- Streamline and the three things you do for it: 1) lock your thumb, 2) squeeze your ears, 3) look down with your whole face.

- Position 11 and the three things you do for it :1) keep your body straight, 2) stay on the surface 3) look down with your whole face when not breathing.

- 3 x streamline + [something] and the rotation method: do the activity then move over across the lane to the other side, and come back and get back in line (setup your lane).

- Lazy puppets -> soldier, soldier -> streamline, and streamline -> position 11 on deck

- How to hold the board for each of the 4 competitive strokes in Individual Medley order.

Once our swimmers are familiar with our set routine and the language we use to queue up different activities, we can start layering in more complicated skills. We can start introducing multi-step actions that require precise and specific body movements that are unique to swimming. Before any of that instruction, before any layered development and rapid learning, we have to establish our routine.

Warm-up Routine and Why

Developmental 1: General Routine

DEVELOPMENTAL 1:

Introductory swim team group

Requirements to get into the group:

25 freestyle with side breathing, arms recovering over the water, face looking down, body straight. 25 backstroke with body straight, arms recovering over the water, and kick near surface.

Minimum age:

5 years old

Maximum age:

13 years old

Goals:

Learn language of swimming: streamline, what the competitive strokes are, learn what we mean by "25's, 50's, 100's," how to swim in a group environment (circle swimming, set up your lane, etc).

Routine:

- Review how you hold the kickboard for each stroke of the individual medley in order.

- 100 IM Kick.

- 2 x 25 position 11.

- Group activities: 2 groups where we do deck work or 3x streamline + [something]

- 50 kick or swim or 25's.

- More group work.

- Game.

In a general sense, this is the daily routine for the first swim team group, or Developmental 1, as I'll refer to it from now on. When we first start in the fall, or in the spring (our second largest new signup period) we strictly adhere to this format. Inside of each activity we follow the same predicable patterns, so the routine is even evident inside the activity. We're going to look at these nestled routines as we move through each section. I want you to think about what you do every day at your practices. Do you use the same words to get kid's attention? Do you like your swimmers to organize in the lane a certain way before you start a set or activity? I like to say, "Alright." To get everyone's attention. That is my cue word to mean, "Stop talking!" Or "Coach Jeff is about to give instructions, be quiet!" I also require that the kids organize their lane a specific way by saying, "Set up your lane."

We get into the habit of "setting up the lane" immediately and spend a longer amount of time ensuring that it happens in the first few weeks of the season. This is a great opportunity for your veteran swimmers to show the new kids what to do, and may demonstrate their leadership skills. Depending on the day, I have at least 1 veteran swimmer in each lane so they can act as the lane leader and help organize. It removes some of the need for the coaches to be physically and verbally directing kids in this order too.

The picture of "set up your lane" shows you how swimmers should move when we move into our next major routine: 3 x streamline + [something]. We'll get into that in a later chapter called "Structure." For now, take a look at your own program and let's hone in on that one specific time that you see a huge influx of new swimmers that are not familiar with your system.

ACTION ITEMS:

WHAT ARE TWO HABITS you have for your swim team coaching?

What do you like done a specific way that you're always showing new swimmers how to do?

Developmental 1: How To Hold Kickboards

There are times with new swimmers where I explicitly do not give them directions. Instead, I want them to look around at their peers and learn from them. If they still don't catch on, I'll repeat the command, "Show me how you hold the board for butterfly kick." And direct my attention and eyes on the new person. They'll look at me panicked, and I'll gesture to everyone else. If there is obvious distress or confusion, I'll physically go over to them and show them exactly what to do, but initially, I'm looking for the problem solving skills. Can you use context clues to understand our commands if you don't grasp the language or can't hear the coach.

We review how to hold the kick board for each competitive stroke in IM order; butterfly, backstroke, breaststroke, and freestyle.

The first routine we do at practice every day for our beginners is to review how to hold the board for the 100 IM kick. We do this for multiple reasons. Here are a few:

- Teaches what the 100 IM order of strokes is

- Teaches how we hold the board for the different strokes. This is vital for beginners as they don't already know, and it is a good consistently safe review for returning people (a chance to succeed right away at practice).

• Allows for discussion about the 100 IM

• What is the order of a 100 IM? We want it to be ingrained and habit: "Fly, back, breast, free."

• Allows for opening about what a 25 is, and what a 50 is.

• Provides a regular expectation for hesitant people that are afraid of group activities (5 - 12 year olds are sometimes scared of leaving their parents and participating in groups).

This routine establishes a regular expectation for the swimmers, and gives us a chance to talk on deck. The kids are used to being quiet and expect some sort of short quiz about swimming. Because they are already following commands, it is a good way to establish structure in delivering directions and sets expectation on how to carry them out. It is a demonstration immediately that the coach will be talking, and the swimmers will be following directions. *In a side note here, we also have a rule that if anyone touches the water before we say it is time to get in they have to do 5 pushups. We enforce this on people even if it is their first day and they don't know the rule. The rule applies to any body part touching the water and any item like a kick board or goggles. I've found it to be a good bonding experience for swimmers because they share stories about how they had to do it the first day too.

We're talking about routine and new swimmers at the start of a season and I'm reminded of my favorite movie of all time: "The Princess Bride." Read this segment from Wikipedia.org:

It is revealed during the course of the story that Roberts is not one man, but a series of individuals who pass the name and reputation to a chosen successor once they are wealthy enough to retire. When the time comes, "Roberts" and his chosen successor sail into port and discharge the crew. Then they hire a new crew, the ex-Roberts staying aboard as first mate and referring to his successor as "Captain Roberts". Once the crew grows accustomed to the new Roberts, the previous captain leaves to enjoy his retirement.

Routine and demonstration work really well with new swimmers when you have a couple of veterans around that know your lingo, that know your habits and routine, and respond quickly and effortlessly to your commands. New swimmers will first look at you, the coach, then at the other swimmers around them to find out what to do. And this is exactly what we want them to do. We want them to not always look at only the coach, but use all the tools around them at their disposal.

Why? Because the pool is a noisy loud environment with lots of different stimuli and they aren't always going to be listening to the coach talk. They're going to be distracted by how it feels to push the water with their hands underwater, how the jets on the side of the pool are warm, and how their hair feels as it clings to their skull when they slowly pull it up out of the water and dip it back in. So many infinite different more interesting things are in the pool than you, and if they miss your brief instructional speech, they'll have to either ask, or figure it out on their own. When we do the 100 IM kick how to hold the kick board, this is a first opportunity for them to learn from their peers (if they truly can't grasp it, or there are no veterans there you should demonstrate).

[kickboard holding pictures]

This is the first routine, and inside of this routine is specific way to actually hold the kickboard for each stroke. This is minutia, but it is important tiny detail. Remember that we have limited time with these swimmers and we want to maximize their learning while at practice. How we hold the board for the first swimming activity we do every single day is important because any action we do in the water should be pointing to a more complicated or difficult skill later on. Every competitive stroke is about the line, finding that long spine and using your core to manipulate your body in a particular way. We hold the kickboard for each stroke specifically to get the body used to that long line immediately. Also, by establishing a specific kickboard holding direction we don't have to review it when we do our 50's or 25's of just kicking, we can simply say: "50 Free kick" and the swimmers know what that means and how they should hold their board.

Butterfly Kick

We hold the board over the head because we want to establish position 11, and putting your face in the water. The kickboard provides a little bit of assistance for beginners when they need to breathe. They can lift their heads up by placing pressure and weight on the arms and the kick board. It interrupts the kick, but eventually as they strengthen we remove the board for butterfly and do the kick in soldier position (hands at the hips, head goes first). At the beginning of practice the swimmers are behind their lanes, and we review and demonstrate how to hold the kickboard for each competitive stroke.

How do you hold the board for butterfly kick? They show us while standing on the deck with their hands over their head, holding the bottom sides of the board and aiming it at the ceiling. The arms should be in position 11.

Backstroke kick

"How do you hold the board for Backstroke Kick?" Press the board flat against your belly and chest. Hold the sides of the board with your elbows bent at right angles (90 degrees) and pull your shoulders back. Body should be mostly straight and it is similar to soldier position. We explicitly (we say it often) tell the swimmers to not hug the board with the forearms laced in front of the board like you're hugging it. We demonstrate that it is wrong by showing and shaking our heads, or saying, "Not like this, but like this." Show the hugging board and then show the holding the sides with your hands and elbows back.

Why do you think we don't "hug" the board for backstroke kick?

I've learned over the years that hugging the board does two dramatic things to the body when you're on your back. 1) It creates a bow, or a banana posture in the body; the hips drop low, the head curls over the cusp of the board, and the feet splash uselessly above or at the surface. 2) It places the whole balance, buoyancy, and sense of safety on the board. The kickboard becomes a literal flotation device instead of a kicking aid. When we hold the sides and use our arms to pull our body up to the board, it places the majority of the balance and floatation on the swimmer's body. The center of buoyancy remains inside the swimmer's body, and makes the kick board less of a floating platform to cling to, and more of a tool to help make floating on your back easier.

I never articulate this to the swimmers, as they're 5 and the concept of buoyancy, center of buoyancy, center of mass, etc is lost on them. But for you, the swim coach, I'm assuming your are aware of these concepts.

I've also found that when we place our hands on the board in this particular fashion for backstroke swimmers revert to this near exact pose when we remove the board. When we kick on our back in soldier position it very closely resembles what we already do every day with the kickboard.

Breaststroke Kick and Freestyle kick Update.

Up until the winter of 2017 I always did the same thing for both breaststroke and freestyle kick with the board. Look at this first picture, and see how the arms are extended over the top of the board. This would require the head to be lifted up out of the water.

I like this position with the board because it allows the swimmers to breathe without any issues. However, it promotes a really bad body position. And, knowing that every action we do in swimming connects to another more race specific skill later on, I've introduced an alternative to kicking with the board for breaststroke and freestyle. Swimmers are now given an option, either hold the board like you do for butterfly, or hold it with the hands at the top of the board and the arms extended above it. If swimmers hold the board at the base, or around the sides at the bottom, then they'll have their face in the water and their body and arms in position 11. They can breathe by lifting their head up in the air as if they're doing a butterfly breath. I've begun calling it "hold the board for breaststroke #1," and "hold the board for breaststroke #2." We review the two options daily to reinforce the differences between the two. I prefer to let the swimmers choose because it allows personal preference and both are valid.

Developmental 1: 100 IM Kick

When I started coaching my own groups I would always start with a 50 freestyle swim or kick. I rationalized it because I thought it would get the swimmers in right away, give them something simple to do, and would "warm" them up for the actual warm up to come. I didn't want to be one of those coaches that wasted time talking, or struggling to cajole kids into the water. If they had a quick easily achievable activity they'd be more likely to get in. It worked! Perhaps from my insistence that they just get in and start, perhaps at the ease of the activity, my swimmers got in the water fast and once in it was easy to start teaching.

This strategy worked great for groups that already had a strong swimming background and were familiar with all the basics, like what is a 25, and what does "IM" mean. When I took over the youngest beginning groups, I needed to teach those basics. Our beginning groups only swam for 45 minutes, and I wanted to maximize that time with a dense purposeful practice. A direction-less 50 FR kick at the beginning was just play time for many of the swimmers, and I figured it would be a good time to begin doing a "warmup" with a learning component.

I started doing a 100 IM kick for everybody right away. In the five minutes before practice started we could review the order of the 100 IM, discuss all the different strokes, cover all the positions and ways to hold a kick board, and once they got in it was an opportunity to do each stroke right away.

"Alright. 100 IM Kick, one length of each stroke. Ready go!"

Literally something I've said over one hundred times, maybe over a thousand at this point. Every day at the beginning of practice after our "how do you hold the kick board" review I say these words. Each one is considered for deliberate effect. "Alright" is the cue word to let swimmers know to listen, and that there are commands or instructions coming. "100 IM kick" follows the pattern of language we use to describe different swims and strokes; 50 free, 100 back k, 4 x 25 on 1:00 Free K w/ fins (we'll get into the format later). "One length of each stroke" lets beginners know what I mean by "100" and is another longer way of saying, "IM." Finally, "ready go" is the cue that lets swimmers know they can start their activity.

Remember that the language we use is extremely important. Coaching is using your words to create specific difficult body motions in people that have limited control over their limbs. We are changing words into action and the ones you choose to use have a profound effect on how well your audience progresses.

The actual kicking.

100 IM Kick is the warmup for the beginners. It is a chance for them to get used to the water, get moving, and to practice both the order of 100 IM, and experiment with every stroke. Coaches spend little time correcting technique unless the swimmer is blatantly doing the wrong kick during their 25's. We'll make

sure they do fly kick on the first 25, and breaststroke kick on the third, but will not spend much, if any time, on fixing poor technique.

I like to think of the warmup as the transition from the outside world into the pool. Have you ever walked into a room full of people you don't know and immediately start following some random person's commands? I know when I go to a conference I'm sitting there with my arms crossed, a scowl on my face, and a mind thinking, "alright bucko, prove to me you're worthy of my attention." Granted, with teachers and coaches that you see on a regular basis there is an inherent authority earned through repeated experience, but if you think to when you were in school did the teachers start with the driest most difficult parts of the lesson right away? No! They small talk, they transition with a recap of last class or comment on the water. There is a period between the outside world and the pool.

For this reason we do not spend a lot of effort and time correcting stroke technique on the first 100 IM kick of the day. We let the swimmers know what each stroke should be for each length, but we're not doing stroke refinement right away. Unless it is not streamlining. That is always worth correcting.

Warmup is the transition from outside to the pool, and I've found it is better to give them space and opportunity to do things well or sloppy in the beginning on their own.

You should focus on:

- Are the swimmers circle swimming: on the right side down, and right side coming back?

• Are the swimmers doing the correct kick each 25?

• Are they holding the kick board correctly for the type of kick they're doing? Backstroke hold for backstroke kick, etc.

• Are they setting up their lane after they finish their 100 IM kick?

WHY 100 IM KICK?

We could have chosen any swim for the first thing. I used to do 50 free swim first with every group. I thought that it was a great way to just get in and go, warm up to the water, and serve as the sever between goofy pre-practice to hard work in practice attitudes. It was okay, but I found 100 IM kick to be much better for a couple of reasons.

Before that a quick story. I was visiting another club's swim team and the coach asked why I let the kids do a 100 IM kick when they couldn't do it perfectly. "What do you mean?" I said. She responded, "Well, I don't let my kids do anything unless they can do it perfectly." I thought it was a very funny thing to say. I responded by saying that I thought giving them a chance to experiment and try out kicking their own way was worth the one 25 they might do wrong. The statement bothered me though; why would we let someone do something they're not good at? My answer is simple, that is how you learn; you try, you attempt, you fail, make a correction, and next time improve. I treat warmup as the kid's opportunity to do things they might not normally do; it is the chance they have to literally do what they've practiced before without me dictating exactly what they should be doing.

Why 100 IM Kick first (even if they don't know how to do breaststroke kick correctly):

With 100 IM kick you give swimmers a chance to practice every kick. It gives us an opportunity to get out of the way and ingrain in their mind the order of the four competitive strokes. We talk before its time to get in how to hold the board for each stroke, another necessary skill that can get overlooked, and we can practice repeating the order of the individual medley in a context outside of a swim meet. The 100 yard length is long enough to satisfy a significant aerobic warmup (especially for beginners), and makes young kids tired enough to need rest while we review the next step in the warm up: 2 x 25 position 11. When they're tired they'll be more quiet and more prone to listen well. The 100 yard distance also works well to serve as a learning opportunity for circle swimming, and how to move in a lane with other swimmers. We can teach how to pass, lane etiquette and how to be passed during the 100.

I coach three different ability groups with over 100 swimmers across them all. The first group, Developmental 1 is 45 minutes. Developmental 2 is 1 hour, and Competitive 1 is 1 hour. I coach back to back from 5:30pm - 8pm; all three groups go in order. Every group starts with 100 IM kick. In competitive 1, we move to a more complicated warmup like this:

- 100 IM Kick

- 100 Swim or Kick

- 50 swim or Kick or drill

- 50 swim or kick or drill

- Question of the Day: 50 something based on answer (yes or no)

- 4 x 25 speedplay (fartlek) on 1:00 kick or swim

I mention this because the 100 IM kick is the same in each of the three groups. That does not change. I find that it is very important to have a consistent activity at the beginning of practice that serves as a mental switch for your participants. Outside the pool they can be social, rowdy, laughing, distracting, or quiet, but once they've done their 100 IM kick, they know that they are at practice and they're there to learn. The physical routine of always doing the 100 IM kick first is a mental and actual cue that says, "practice has started. Time to start putting effort and attention into learning."

ACTION ITEMS

WHAT IS YOUR DAILY introduction to swimming practice? What do you do every day? Maybe this is not a specific item like 100 IM kick (though I strongly encourage you to use it), but instead a 200 something, or a 50 something.

What are the multiple benefits of doing your beginning routine?

_____
_____

Developmental 1: 2 x 25 Position 11

———

"Who can tell me the three things that you should do for streamline?"

1) Lock your thumb

2) Squeeze your ears

3) Look down

I'll ask this question every single day to the first developmental group because we want them to establish it as a habit before every single activity that the swimmers do. While we wait for the last two people to finish their 100 IM kick, we start quizzing the swimmers on the three things for streamline. Doing this serves a bunch of different purposes. It gives the swimmers something to do while they wait, it is a habit and expected round of questions (we always ask every day the three things you should do for streamline), it establishes a routine of listening and quizzing, it reinforces the core tenets of effective streamlines, and it is a good primer for new people. It is also literally the next skill that they will do; streamline, then position 11 the rest of the way (25).

After the 100 IM kick we always do 2 x 25s of position 11.

"Alright, next we're going to do 2, 25's of position 11. Who can tell me what you do first?"

- Answer: streamline.

"Yes, streamline! Remember, streamline first, then do position 11 the rest of the way." Then demonstrate what it looks like on deck while standing.

Encourage veteran participants to go first so new people can see what they're doing. I like to let them "figure" it out instead of going into overt detail with this drill as we will do it every day and it is extremely difficult to do well.

After the first 25, we wait for everyone to finish and then ask the following question, every single day. Again we want to establish this as habit, as so clear and obvious that swimmers don't need to think about it.

"What are the three things to do position 11 well?"

1) Keep your arms straight

2) Stay at the surface

3) Look down (when not breathing)

Why do we focus on these three specific things for this drill?

Like streamline we want to distill down to the most basic actionable steps someone can take to most effectively improve swimming. Our ultimate goal is better ability I all 4 competitive strokes (butterfly, backstroke, breaststroke, freestyle). Position 11 is a great drill to establish long extension of the arms, good neutral body position and posture, and teaches the concept of buoyancy and depth correction to beginners in a subtle way. Remembering that intention, look at the breakdown of why we review these three things for position 11 every day.

"Keep your arms straight"

Yes, even when lifting the head up to breathe, keep the arms straight and in the full extension position (in front of the shoulders while laying down, or on deck above the shoulders). This is extremely difficult to do and will require lots of practice and effort particularly from the kick and a fast breath. We use this as a key word or phrase because it is a target, it is the end goal of doing the drill well. It makes the drill more challenging.

Beginners will scull, or doggy paddle when they breathe. Initially we don't correct it with beginners because the drill is so difficult, but we reinforce every day that keeping the arms straight during the drill is expected. Because we do this every day, and because we review this step every day, we often do not stop swimmers mid 25 to correct failure unless they have been with the team a long time or if they're getting "lazy" (people that can do it but choose not to that day).

Keeping your arms straight focuses on the long extension and the long reach and line. Every stroke hits this fully extended arm position and doing this drill reinforces it as a goal target with every stroke. We do it every day because if you can maintain position 11 in a drill, you can get to it, and reference it later on when teaching the strokes. When you're teaching fly, you can say, reach to position 11 with every stroke, then pull underwater. Or breaststroke, you can say, shoot to position 11 and glide. It gives a target body position reference point that you can use later on to effectively communicate and give a visual and mental cue.

Keeping your arms straight when you breathe, and when you are not kicking, is difficult. It is not easy, so we target it, and use it as one of the three key factors to doing the drill well.

"Stay at the surface"

What happens when you do a front float and then you only lift your head up and leave it up. What happens to your body, your feet? They sink! Yes, you're right, we have had our swimmers do this. About once a month we tell the kids to do a front float and lift your head up. Don't do anything else, just float, then lift up your head. I ask, "What happens?" It is obvious; you sink. How can you stay at the surface then when you breathe during position 11? Well, you kick faster a little bit and you breathe faster! Stay at the surface is a target key point of position11 because it requires a lot of smaller pieces to accomplish. You need to kick faster, breathe quickly, and re-balance your body after the disruptive up lifted head breath. To stay at the surface when lifting your head up to breathe is not easy.

You'll often see swimmers keep their arms straight, breathe during position 11, and then immediately sink underwater and banana shape their body to get back to the surface. The challenge of doing position 11 well is to keep the body at the surface through the breath and immediately after. When done well, the skills required to stay at the surface translate directly to effective competitive stroke swimming: fast breath, maintained body line, buoyant body position.

Stay at the surface is a challenge and a goal, a target. We say this as a key factor of position 11 because it translates well to every other stroke.

"Look down"

If you coach swimming, you're probably tired of saying this over and over again, but it needs to be done. You simply have to reinforce this every opportunity you can. This is another opportunity to introduce this concept early and often. Aim the head down when not breathing and maintain a neutral position at the surface while kicking with arms at full extension. We say "aim the whole face down to the bottom." The crown of the head should point forward or the direction you're moving, while the nose and forehead aim down or perpendicular to the floor.

When a swimmer breathes, they start to sink, but if they immediately get their head down, they'll re-balance their body and stay near the surface. The head down immediately translates directly to good habit formation for breaststroke and butterfly.

Look down is a key word target phrase because it is the struggle of all coaches to get the kids to look down and not where they're going; it is faster.

ACTION ITEMS

WHAT KEY PHRASES DO you reinforce every day at the beginning of practice? Do you do a specific short distance skill drill every day like Position 11?

Why do you think it is important to repeat something daily?

How do you make streamline a habit, an ingrained portion, of every swim?

Build a Practice

Structure: Basic building blocks

3X SL+ [SOMETHING]

When I first started coaching a real USA Swimming team it was as an assistant. I didn't have to think about what we did every day, I just followed what the lead coach decided we would do. I didn't have to consider who I was working with, or what exactly we needed to work on and in what order. No, I could show up every day and simply follow the written practice. It was a great way to start learning how to coach. Because I wanted to learn how to do things well I asked a lot of questions and did my best to learn the structure of why we did things in what particular order. My lead coach basically had a similar format: warm-up, drill set, aerobic set, and then sprint set. There was some deviation, but in general that was the process that we followed each day.

When I started coaching on my own, I started with the same format but adjusted for more limited ability. We would do a warm-up, a drill set, and then an aerobic set that built upon the drills we did. I'm sure most of you reading this book have a similar format or general structure that you follow.

After two years of coaching with the mid level age group swimmers I took over the beginning portion of the swim team. I was well equipped to handle the beginners because I was already running the swim lesson program that fed into it, and was coaching the group that the developmental program in turn fed into. There was just this gap between lessons and advanced swimmers that I needed to learn how to teach. From this new challenge I waded into the format that revolutionized my coaching and drastically improved our swim lesson program as well.

I believe the foundation for how swim teams should operate is to allow multiple opportunities to attempt a new skill with targeted specific feedback.

We want to give our swimmers as much of the coach's attention as possible and provide feedback or "coaching" that makes the swimmers better faster. One of the best ways you can do that is to do something over and over for very short distances (under 8 seconds of activity) and then each round that the person does an activity give them specific feedback on what they did well and how they can improve the next time. If you can also give them two or three target skills that will allow them to accomplish complicated motions and movements the better. In order to fulfill those requirements we came up with this general format: three times, plus a streamline, then do an activity. In shorthand: 3x SL + [something]

That is the foundation of our most effective teaching moments. There are so many wonderful things baked into this simple short distance phrase that it has come to dominate a full half of all practices and is the bedrock of our swim lesson program. The beauty of the setup is that we can swap in so many different skills and the format, the structure and scaffolding, is all in place and understood by the swimmers. Here are a few examples of things we do:

- 3 x SL + 3 Free

- 3 x SL + 3 free + flip

- 3 x SL with no kick + 1 (11, Y, Eat, and Reach while floating) no kick) Short version once details understood: 3 x SL + 1 (11, Y, E, 11).

- 3 x SL + 1 fly stroke no k

- 3 x SL to flags on back

- 3 x SL + 5 FR + 1 Breath + flip (no breathing on stroke 1 or 5 or before the flip)

You can see from the listed things above that most things are very similar (go three times, do a streamline and then do something (often 3 of those "somethings"). Again, the exciting and wonderful part of this is that the framework is the same and we can swap in any number of skills! You can virtually shoehorn any skill in the water into this format and get some excellent learning and progress in your participants! We deliberately keep the distances short so the coach can see it all. The streamline is immediate (and it is one of the primary goals of the groups I coach: establish streamline as a habit) and I can give direct feedback on the streamline with each attempt in addition to the actual swimming skill done. Heck, we even do this as just "3x streamline with free kick" to practice streamline. Including streamline as a listed skill first each time establishes it as a component of the actually swimming. We don't "assume" that they're going to streamline because we're working with beginners and we need to be explicit in every activity giving exact descriptions of what will occur to do something successfully.

Explain how this works.

3 x SL + [something]

Everyone does the listed activity including the streamline three times. We rotate who goes, and follow the rotation method:

Set up
your Lane

1st person in Right
corner
2nd person in Left
corner
_____
Leave the middle
open

Follow the red lines on the picture. We "set up the lane" so we can effectively do this format of activity: 3 x SL + [something]. Each person in your lane (up to 5 usually for time's sake if you can) does the activity, then they get back in line. After they complete the activity they move directly across the lane and then can do anything they want getting back in line. They then wait for their turn. Yes. There will be a moment where they are not directly doing an activity, and this is okay. You can get 3 repetitions in under 5 minutes once your group knows the format. In fact, a good group of 4 will do this 3 times in under 3 minutes once they know the activity and the setup. Your job is to then watch the swimmers as they take their turns and give immediate feedback limited to the activity they're doing (don't give fly feedback when they're doing freestyle). The lane goes until everyone has gone 3 times. If you have a slow lane, let the fast lanes do an extra round or two.

When does the next person go?

Swimmers can take their turn once the way is clear, and I often respond to questions of "can I go now?" with, "is the way clear? Did they move to the side?" they reply, "yes," and then I say, "then go."

Have swimmers wait until the person ahead of them have moved across the lane and into the oncoming traffic side. We circle swim down the right, so when the person ahead crosses into the left side of the lane, then the person ahead can go. We ask that swimmers keep the same order so there is no fighting or problems with whose turn it is or who goes first or too many times while others haven't completed their rounds. They then go until everyone has gone at least 3 times.

Why only 3 times?

Initially because it was because of time constraints. I wanted to get at least everyone through the rounds and we split everyone up into two groups, so we had to do the same activity twice. When I first started doing these activities it was to accommodate our small pool with a large number of kids. If you remember I coach 40 kids out of a 4 lane 20 yard pool. It is shallow: 3.5 ft and deepest is 4.5 ft. To give the kids a good learning experience we split the group in half and sent one group to the deep end and another to the shallow. Both groups would sometimes do the same thing, or something different. When they were different it was like they were doing stations; an activity at each location that was different. I found that I wanted to keep the time limit down to about 5 minutes in each group and 3 times was short enough to explain the activity, set up the lanes, and then have the kids do it enough times to improve and get feedback. When we got more familiar with the setup we would do 5 times. We still do 3 times because it is quick, but provides a good number of attempts to figure out and improve on an activity.

The first attempt is to make sure you're doing it right, the second to improve on any major mistakes and the third to refine small improvements. If you go up to 5 times you are verging on the boring and should be wary with true beginners. Typically we only go 5 times with the more advanced groups because they're more interested in perfection than stimulation and interest, though we limit the 5 times to once or twice a practice because it is really stretching out the attention capabilities of deliberate practice and mental energy. So three times is the sweet spot of attempts.

Why is SL (streamline) always first?

Remember that we're working with developmental swimmers, or beginners. They're not familiar yet with all the lingo and jargon that comes with swimming. We want to be as explicit in every word and thing we do in our practices; both because we want to be efficient, but also because we want to only provide and expose the swimmers to correct ways of doing things. It does not behoove us or the swimmers to do something 'wrong' or omit something because we're being lazy. Then your age group coach has to retrain and correct it later on.

Streamline is aways first because it is another opportunity to establish it as a habit for the first initial action when doing anything. You'll see that it is the constant. I bet you can guess what my biggest age group and senior level swimming pet peeve of mine is. Go ahead. Guess. I know you know; STREAMLINE! OH MY GOD! It is like nails on chalkboards, like seeing blood, like imagining someone else's pain, like thinking of falling off your bike. Ugh. It makes me crazy to see people that once had a streamline habit push off with a half, lazy not-streamline. Lock the thumb, squeeze the ears and look down! You can do it, you did it a thousand times with me in the developmental program!

We want to establish streamline as a habit. Include "SL" or streamline as a part of these short distance activities helps establish it as a fundamental skill. We're not just doing three strokes of freestyle, but we're doing a good quality streamline (with all three things) and then also the three strokes.

Why short distance?

I briefly touched on this earlier; why we only do three strokes or short distances. There is one reason that we first started doing it: we split our group in half and used both ends of the 20 yard pool. In order to not run into each other we were limited in only going 1/2 way. Our initial reason was out of necessity limited by our pool, but we continue to follow this format even when we have access to bigger spaces. Here are a few reason why we continue with the shorter distances.

- We want to limit the time spent attempting a new physical skill.

- I found through my experience that it is easier for beginners to attempt something with a high degree of focus and intent (just a streamline and a few strokes is easier than a whole 25).

- It is easier for the coach to see the whole attempt (at the activity) and then give immediate feedback. Each attempt is only about 5-10 seconds.

- The coach can see two or three people going at the same time. They are always leaving in the same place in the lane and only going a short way away, generally staying within the coach's field of view.

- Physically less demanding for weak swimmers.

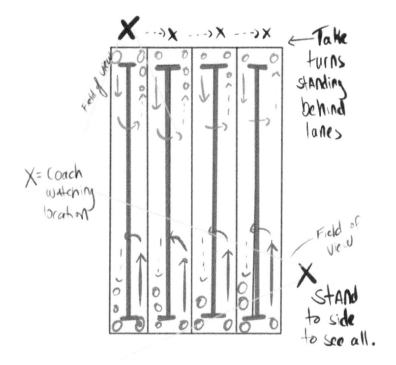

When we limit the amount of time that someone spends attempting a new challenging skill it reduces mental fatigue. With a quick short attempt and then immediate feedback we allow the swimmer an opportunity to self evaluate, and then within a few minutes they get to attempt the same skill armed now with a corrective action plan (assuming they got feedback from the coach).

Because we are doing a very short distance with a low physical and endurance demand on the swimmer they don't have to worry about swimming a long time or breathing (usually). Removing the stress of a longer swim and the stress of struggling to breath allows for a more relaxed stroke. The lower physical demand also allows swimmers to attempt new skills without getting tired. They can attempt the skill without "saving" or struggling to breathe and then do it wrong or poorly. I've found that the short distance removes much of the bad habit compromises that swimmers create when they are moving long distances without correct technique. The short distance has the added bonus of the coach immediately there giving feedback to smooth out those bad habits right when they happen; instead of waiting till they finish the 25, or screaming and yelling to get their attention.

I particularly like how easy it is to see 15 kids doing the same activity and give them all at least 1 or 2 interactions of specific targeted feedback on the streamline and the skill. My swimmers are in the habit of looking at me immediately after each attempt because I so consistently give them feedback after each attempt (you'll need to train them to do this by calling their name, telling them to stop, or waving them down after each attempt). The kids I work with celebrate the thumbs ups that I hand out when they do something really well, or near perfection. In these short distance sets we are expecting very high quality swimming; as near perfect as you can get. I can also place myself at the side of the lane (see graphic) or behind each lane and watch everyone go once in like a mini 'test.'

Remember to give high quality feedback for each swimmer every time (as possible). Briefly summarizing high quality feedback: say something they did well that I sin line with your version of excellent swimming technique, give them a specific thing to improve upon, hopefully that is in line with some very simple repeated goals (3 things for streamline for example). Limit your feedback to one or two items. If someone fails spectacularly it is fine to list off everything they did wrong to let them know, but only give them one or two actionable changes for their next future attempt. If we say too many things to fix it is overwhelming (see podcasts about "the one thing" with Meighan Julbert, Karis Mount, Dominic Latella, and Jeff Grace).

———————————

ACTION ITEMS

———————————

WHAT ARE SOME ACTIVITIES that you can do immediately after a streamline, but no more than 1/2 way down the pool? Can you think of a way to incorporate the flags or yellow buoys into your instruction as targets?

Do you already use short distance skill work in your swim team?

Can you do demanding drills in a shorter distance so you can give better feedback?

Is it better to do 25's and let swimmer's do a drill wrong multiple times without correction, or should they do a streamline and one or two iterations of the drill then stop?

Replaceable Parts

———

S wapping into 3 x SL + [something]: What are those "somethings?"

Earlier I mentioned that we have a framework, or a scaffolding for our practices to follow. In the previous chapter, "Structure: Basic Building Blocks" I reviewed in detail the "3 x SL + [something] structure. But this book is about how to create fun and effective swim practices. How can you be interesting and entertaining by doing the "same thing every day?"

Replace your parts. Yes, your structure, your rails like a train's tracks will be the same. You're moving along a set course like a road with yellow and white lines so you don't veer off into a ditch. Think about how you can substitute your "something" with what you want to work on.

Over the years I've come up with a huge list of different activities we can do for every stroke. Many of those things are small essential parts of each stroke separated out into actionable, digestible bits.

One of the main goals for the first developmental group is to teach good freestyle. I mean freestyle with side breathing keeping the face touching the water and no lifting forward. I mean freestyle with arms that reach to a full extension and maintain a straight body position.

How do you get to that advanced level of freestyle when your beginners, people that have just joined the team after a tryout, are swimming with wild flailing arms, side breathing that is not always perfect, and when they get tired after twenty minutes reverting back to head lifting body bending banana madness?

You see, we let swimmers onto the team when they can swim one length of freestyle with side breathing, and even then it doesn't need to be perfect. That means many of these beginners cannot do 8 x 25's of freestyle with good technique. They can usually do 1 or 2. So how do we train that better swimming ability? We do shorter distances with plenty of rest where they get specific targeted feedback. Then we do a 25, or a 50 so they get a chance to demonstrate for a longer distance what we just practiced in our small groups.

SL + 3 FR is a specific effort to see all of that excellent freestyle without the panic of breathing, without the struggle to keeping it going for 25 yards, without worrying about whether the person can maintain that level of mental willpower the whole time.

We've applied that same thinking to every other stroke.

How can we break the stroke down into easy achievable parts that require focus on one or two different steps? How do we take breastroke and turn it into four different 3 x SL + [something]'s?

Breaststroke parts:

- Glide (position 11)

- Arms, (11, Eat, 11)

- Kick

We can break each of those parts into small and smaller chunks. Take the Breaststroke kick for example. We do these "3x" things:

○ Flex

○ Lift and flex

○ Open and closed with straight legs

So the first time a swimmer is introduced to BR kick, it isn't as the whole kick, it is as a streamline with the legs straight and the feet in the flex position.

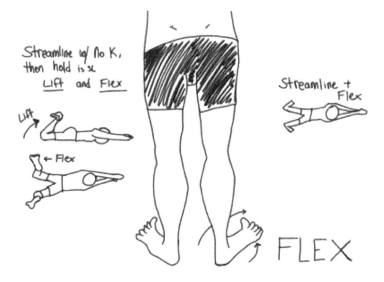

Look at the picture on the far right, swimmers push off in streamline, and also flex the whole time. This is a small replaceable part, or chunk, for a 3 x SL + FLEX activity. The next step in the build up to breaststroke kick is (looking at the left of the picture now) 3 x SL + Lift and Flex. The swimmers lift their feet above their knees and then flex all while in streamline. They hold for 3 seconds in the lifted and flex position. It is the primer to doing a breaststroke kick.

What small chunks, or replaceable parts can you think of to put into a breaststroke progression using the 3 x SL + [something] format?

When I'm making a practice and looking at a stroke that I want to work on I'm thinking about what smaller pieces do I need to break this complicated swimming skill into so most of the swimmers can do it? I know that not everyone is able to do a great perfect breaststroke kick. I know that. Yet, my goal is to get as many swimmers as possible in the direction of learning that incredibly difficult skill.

I know what a good breaststroke kick looks like. Using 3 x SL + [something] to practice those smaller parts of the whole maximizes the framework and the familiar routine but with different specifics so as to stay effective and interesting.

What I find amazing is how excited swimmers get with doing "fun" activities inside the 3 x SL + [something] format.

I love hearing a cheer when I'll say we're doing 3 x SL + 3 free, and a swimmer will ask, "can we do a flip at the end?" I'll say yes, and I'll see some boys do the fist pump "yeah!" move, and the girls will jump and clap. For them, the added difficulty and excitement of doing a flip at the end of their deliberate practice gives them significant satisfaction. I'm happy because they are practicing flip turns without realizing it, and they're happy because they love flips and playing in the water.

Another point of excitement that I savor is when they celebrate after getting a thumbs up. After each attempt a swimmer does they get feedback about how they did. Most of the time I say they did something well, and give them a target to improve the next round.

For example, "You did a good streamline with all three things, but you lifted your head up when you did your three free strokes. Next time look down while you swim." If they do it correct or well on the next round I give them a thumbs up and I always laugh when I see them celebrate with a smile, a beaming splash slap, or my favorite: a celebratory fist / elbow pull back with the silent "Yes!"

While our routine, our framework, "3 x SL + [something] remains the same the small variations provide a familiar playground for the swimmers to interact with. We can do wild things like "5 x SL with FLY K + 3 FR strokes" or 2 x (2 x SL BAD *do something wrong*) and (2 x SL + Flip when you get to surface). The frame, the basic structure like a metal beam in a building remains the same but we change small details to make it interesting and dynamic.

This allows for great flexibility in what we do in our small groups with a monstrously quick roll out. Whenever we introduce a new skill, drill, or activity it rests within the bedrock of "3 x SL + [something]."

What to substitute in for "something?"

I'm going to give you a list of things we do in our practices in the hopes that you'll find something useful and beneficial to your program. If you subscribe to the Developmental Swim Practices at https://gum.com/practices then you'll be familiar with many of these activities and skill breakdowns.

List of 3 x SL + ...

- 3 x SL + FLIP

- 3 x SL + 3 FR

- 5 x SL + 5 FR + 1 breath on 2, 3, 4 + Flip

- 3 x SL, 1 at surface, 1 at middle depth, 1 at bottom

- 3 x SL + 3 FR + 18 K on side

- 3 x SL + 5 K in 11 + 1 arm stroke

- 3 x SL + 2 x (5 k in 11 + 1 FR)

- 3 x SL on BK on surface

- 3 x SL on BK underwater

- 3 x SL + through hula hoop

- 3 x SL + 3 BK after the flags

- 3 x SL + 3 Bk after flags, then roll over and do front flip.

- 5 x Fall down underwater, lay on back and push off in SL

- 5 x Flip first at wall + SL on back underwater

- 3 x SL + NO Kick

- 3 x SL + Flex

- 3 x SL + Lift and Flex, then hold 4 seconds

- 3 x SL + 11, Eat, 11

- 3 x SL + 2x (11, Eat and breath, 11) NO KICK

- 3 x SL + 1 x (11, Eat and breath, 11) in position 11 do 1 BR K

- 3 x SL + fly kick

- 3 x SL + 1 Fly motion, no kick. Ok for arms to push body backwards

- 3 x SL + 2 FLY strokes no kick

- 3 x SL with fly kick + 1 FLy stroke with one kick Right as hands go from airplane to 11.

- 3 x SL + Ready position and Load (lift hip up and let water flood lower back).

- 3 x SL + 3 FR 1 arm only

- 3 x SL + 3 BK 1 arm only.

- 3 x SL + HLBw/R with three hips up

Aerobic conditioning

This book is about fun and effective tactics for developmental and beginner age group practices. This section is not about providing a proper training program for elite athletes that have been swimming multiple years, or are in high school, or training for state, nationals, and the Olympics. This section looks at how we provide an aerobic conditioning element to our practices for beginner and intermediate swimmers.

We do yardage. It may seem like the whole practice is short distances and targeted skill work, but we also swim. We do 100's, 50's, and 25's on intervals and as a part of sets. One of my favorite sets is 3 x { 1 x 100 Kick, 1 x 200 swim}. I love the 200 as a distance for swimmers that can hold their stroke together while still doing flip turns and streamlines. This isn't a set for the developmental 1 group, but it would be appropriate for a third level group where swimmers have those habits ingrained.

There is a place for a challenging aerobic set like doing 10 x 50's or 10 x 100's. That is a good thing! There are good reasons to do long, boring sets. One of my favorite sets that I use throughout a season is a 30 minute swim, or a 15 minute swim. There is absolutely a good reason to swim for a long time to incite boredom. Maybe you're looking to see how long your group can maintain effective swimming. Maybe you're looking to see where they start to fail first. Maybe you want to give them exposure to longer swims in a safe setting.

This last week we had every day of practice canceled due to snow, extreme cold, building shut downs, and an ice storm. On the first day back everyone showed up after a full week off. For our Developmental 2 group we did a long boring set of 600 yards after our typical warm-up. It was a way to manage their hyperactive behavior and to reestablish a sense that we weren't just playing games but swimming well.

There are great reasons to do long boring sets, but do them sparingly and on occasion. Be careful. We can get just as lazy as our swimmers skipping streamlines and letting body lines falter.

My question to you as the coach would be, is your set providing an opportunity for your swimmers to deliberately practice a specific skill beyond swimming for aerobic conditioning alone?

You might be saying, of course, yes. Look at your swimmers during one of your sets where you do not explicitly give them a target skill or focus, or goal. Are they streamlining with their hands locked and elbows tight against their ears? Probably not. Are they flipping at the wall, streamlining on their back for a short distance with immediate fly kicks, turning taking a stroke then breathing on their second or third stroke? I doubt it.

Most times when given a set without direction your swimmers will default to their lazy swimming habits. They'll skip the tight streamline because it isn't regularly enforced. They'll wiggle their core because maintaining a rigid spine and breath takes mental effort. They'll glide into turns, breathe on the first stroke and move their head with wild deviation because what you assume they should always do isn't explicitly stated.

With swimming and children participants we are fighting entropy.

Again, from James Clear https://jamesclear.com/entropy:

"It is the natural tendency of things to lose order. Left to its own devices, life will always become less structured. Sand castles get washed away. Weeds overtake gardens. Ancient ruins crumble. Cars begin to rust. People gradually age. With enough time, even mountains erode and their precise edges become rounded. The inevitable trend is that things become less organized.

[...]

But because the universe naturally slides toward disorder, you have to expend energy to create stability, structure, and simplicity. Successful relationships require care and attention. Successful houses require cleaning and maintenance. Successful teams require communication and collaboration. Without effort, things will decay."

Swimmers in a long set will begin to falter unless we provide them with constant feedback, guided direction, and aim like a spotlight on their behavior. We need to be engaged as coaches to tend our gardens against entropy and decay: the loss of deliberate good technique.

So yes, provide long convoluted sets with multiple yards and difficult intervals, but do it with an eye for attention, deliberate practice, and the attention span of your swimmers.

You will not be able to get as much out of 10 x 50's with a beginning group as you will with a more advanced one.

Adjust your yardage to be appropriate for the ability level of your swimmers. Adjusting the yardage of a long multi-step set for a beginning group is not an effective way to run a practice. If you have all of your 11-13 year olds doing the same practice, regardless of ability level, but with different distances the beginners will be left behind, they'll make lots of mistakes, they'll find the practices boring, too difficult, and like they're ignored. They'll quit.

Some teams will do 10 x100 on 2:00; beginners should do 10 x 75 on same interval.

Do you think the beginners will streamline well? Think the extra rest will make their strokes better? With coaching, they will, but I would say this is a very ineffective way at teaching those skills. Better to change their practice entirely where they're *taught* those skills in a way that gives them a chance to do them well on their own, then layered into ever more challenging distances and sets.

Yes. There is a place for aerobic conditioning, but it should be done considering "is this set appropriate for this ability level?"

Shorter "sets" after deliberate practice

I like to have a pattern to my practices. We begin with a skill introduction, then move onto a longer aerobic set where we practice those same skills that we just spent significant time and feedback teaching. We'll do some drill work, or short distance skill training, then an aerobic set which provides an opportunity to demonstrate that same skill in a longer swimming environment. If we worked on streamlines we'll do a set of 25's where swimmers are expected to streamline well. That is their goal and focus. If we do a series of drills working on rotation, we'll do a set of 50's or 25's that explicitly allow for swimming freestyle or backstroke to connect the drill to the swim.

I also like to work in opposites to sets so that swimmers get a chance to recover, or swim with mindless effort so when we return to the portion of the set that connects to the drill and skill work they have a fresh mind.

For example, I like doing a lot of kick sets as a part of the swimmer's aerobic conditioning. Take a look at this progression:

Two groups:

1) 3 x SL + 11, E, 11

2) 3 x flip first + SL on back to flags underwater.

Together:

3 x {

1 x 100 FR K w/ flip turns and SL on back (mindless effort small attention needed on flip turns).

4 x 25 BR 2 strokes FR swim the rest of the 25. (Huge deliberate effort on those first 2 BR strokes and not difficult FR the rest).

}

The set I've described above is a good 45 minutes of aerobic swimming, deliberate skill work on breaststroke and flip turns, then a set that provides aerobic opportunity with the 100 kick, and skill work on both breaststroke and flip turns. My goal is excellent BR during the 2 strokes every 25. I know that working with kids they can only aim their attention at something for a short amount of time, and only when it is interesting. They need to run around work out their energy and distraction and be wild sometimes. This gives them a chance to do that. And when I'm coaching, I'm on the deck reminding them before every 25 what I want them to focus on.

Give a rousing speech. Speak individually with each swimmer about their BR. Aim your attention at what matters and you'll see within the set effort directed at what you want them to do.

Action Items:

Look at your last three practices. How many opportunities did you give for deliberate practice of a specific skill within "set?" For this, deliberate practice can mean specific attention to a particular way of swimming, maybe counting strokes, streamlines to a specific target distance, or swimming a stroke with attention on what your drills before it had them focus on.

Justify a long boring set.

How can you make that set achieve your goals, but not lead to mindless swimming?

Is there a place for long boring sets?

How can you create an aerobic set that also provides opportunity for deliberate practice?

Games

Find all of the swim games we use at practice and swim lessons here: https://swimminglessonsideas.com/games/

This is the hardest chapter for me to write. I wrote a whole book on "How to Create Fun and Effective Swim Games," and I still don't think I did the subject justice. It is difficult to explain, to describe and show without having you on the deck with me while the practices are going on. I'm going to give you a few examples, but ultimately say that the creative use of games and group activities that provide an opportunity to be interesting yet make sure participants are putting deliberate practice into quality swimming is a great way to make your practices fun and effective.

They are ways to test how good your instruction and training has been, and they're excellent ways to see where the group is as a whole. If you see a lot of sloppy swimming and confused looks in a game that relies on stuff they don't know or have never done before it can tell you what you need to introduce or work on my as a coach. If your game is too easy then you can start making your practices more challenging.

I've given my assistant coaches multiple opportunities to come up with their own games. Sometimes they are very conservative or wild and crazy. Each time I want them to have a chance to experiment without judgment from my part, and as we move through their games I give them feedback on what went well, things I would change, and do my best to lead them through the process so they can create a game on their own without too many initial stumbling blocks.

Most recently over the Winter break we had a lot of people gone and those that were coming every day were the same kids. It would have been boring to continue doing the same things every single day so we took the opportunity to experiment. I let my assistant coach come up with a different game for the Developmental 2 group every day based on what we were doing in the Developmental 1 group (whose practice I wrote and comes immediately before the Dev. 2 group). She did a wonderful job of coming up with a great game using this simple formula:

- Who is this game for?

- What is the main skill I want to work on?

- How can we do it by making it more difficult, or put up a roadblock, or be interesting?

- How are you going to explain the activity/game in the clearest most concise way?

Here are some things that the she came up with:

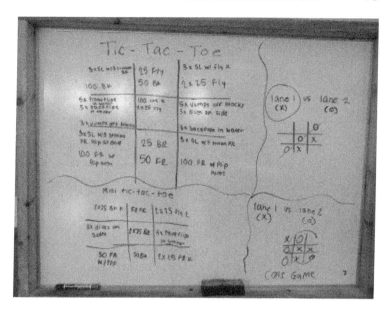

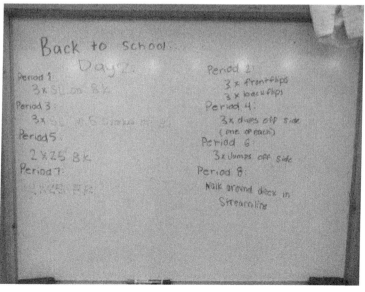

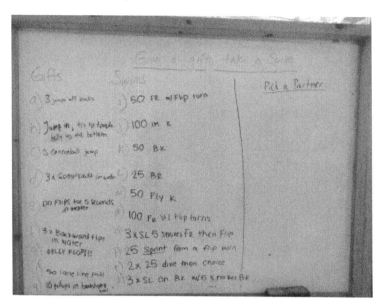

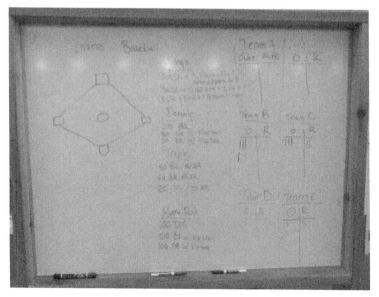

I want to look specifically at the "Tic Tak Toe" game.

What you see in the picture, the first of the ones displayed here, is the final revision after playing the game four times through. We ironed out some of the rough parts and made it a bit easier. If you're interested in the details about how to play the game you can find that information here: https://swimminglesson-sideas.com/2019/01/10/swimming-game-tic-tac-toe/

The first version of this game had a lot more complicated and difficult swimming skills inside each box. The coach didn't know exactly how to match up the ability level of the swimmers, the amount of effort they would put into doing things well, and how we could enforce good quality swimming against the fun and racing aspect of the game.

Basically, two teams are competing on the same board to fill in X's and O's before the other. If both team choose to do the middle square, then the team that finishes it first gets that box. We struggled coaching this because we didn't want one team sitting there doing nothing while the other did their activity, so there was a bit of a rush through the skills and activities. What were we going to do when both teams did a 200 Free and saw that the other team did it too but faster? What if they cheated? Who got the X or O in that square? We had to iron out those details as we went.

Take a look at the last picture, the game "Baseball." This game is an interesting challenge for the coach because it makes you think about the things your swimmers know how to do already. What you see here is a revised version of the game after playing it three times. The premise is that each lane or team gets a chance to pick an activity. Activities are seperated into four tiers with a Home Run being the most difficult, and a Single being achievable by almost everyone. The team does the activity, and if they do it well without getting disqualified (no streamline, wrong stroke, no flip turn, etc) then the team gets that type of hit. If they fill the bases and send people to home they get a run. If they get 3 out (when they do an activity and fail it, you wipe the bases and start a new round).

For a coach, the challenge is how well do you know your group? What skills are quick, simple and easy to do with little instruction, but require lots of deliberate practice. It provides a filter to what skills you're going to choose for your group. You have to make it appropriate yet interesting and challenging enough that the swimmers have to strive to succeed.

The "baseball" game and the "tic-tak-toe" game are not anything revolutionary. In fact, they're amusing wrappers around stuff that we would already be doing at practice, but we've gamified elements of swim practice to make it more interesting. In order to earn points, or let their team advance, swimmers need to do things well, and when you call them out for sloppy or wrong swimming they remember all the training, feedback, and guidance you've given them in previous practices. They improve!

Here are a few more pictures of games you might enjoy:

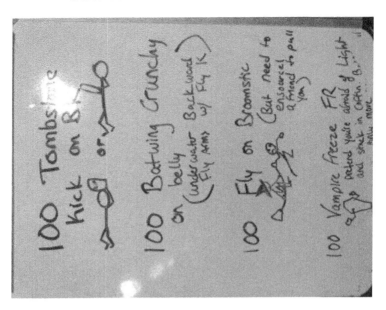

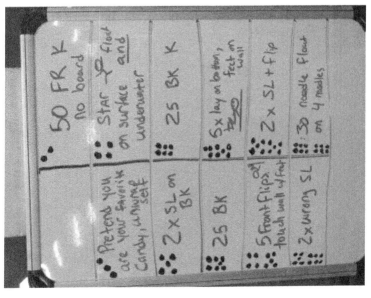

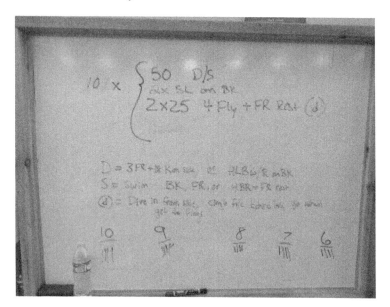

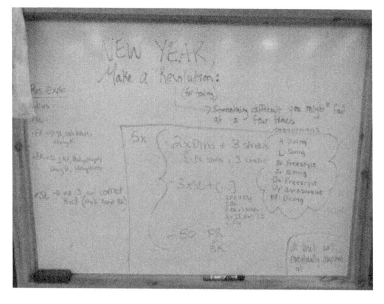

Find all of the swim games we use at practice and swim lessons
here: https://swimminglessonsideas.com/games/

Scientific Artistry

Strechting: Just beyond ability

FINDING DELIBERATE practice is the second chapter of this book. Fun and effective swim practices are about allowing multiple opportunities for deliberate practice during your practices. My goal Is that by now you have a firm foundation upon which you can have your own fun and effective swim practices. Deliberate practice is our ultimate goal, and stretching, where the art of reaching for something just beyond your capability is the skill target that we should have when we're considering things to do.

I think of "stretching" as providing a skill or activity that is just beyond the grasp or concept of my swimmers. If I'm working with a seven-year-old who only knows how to swim freestyle, then when I'm teaching him how to do flip turns, the stretching portion of that is a flip combined with the streamline on your back underwater.

For that seven-year-old, they may lack the body awareness and physical ability to do a forward flip, land the feet on the wall, and push off in streamline with a flat back.

They may not even be able to do a flip without holding their nose.

The trick of excellent coaching, and effective coaching, is to find that unique ability level in each individual and provide them an opportunity to practice or improve on something just beyond their skill level.

With this seven-year-old mind, I may focus on making sure that the feet go directly above the head during the flip. This would allow the swimmer to aim their attention at a single skill instead of overwhelming them with multiple things they need to improve.

Reaching, or stretching, is something that with a few rounds of deliberate practice a swimmer would be able to learn, or demonstrate.

Most people might be familiar with the term "moving the goal posts" in regards to this topic. It is an appropriate one, especially because I feel that I'm constantly dragging in front of my swimmers new and ever more challenging skills.

Once they master something there is something else for them to work. If we continue with this seven-year-old practicing flip turns, once they have mastered a flip we would move on to foot placement on the wall, and the power triangle. From there we might focus on how far to flip, as a flip turn is a half flip, followed by how we push off in streamline and where we should put our hands. At every step there is another more complicated progressive improvement to master. The goalposts keep moving.

I'm not a particularly outgoing person. I'm shy in group settings and get crippling anxiety before I have to speak in front of large groups of people that I don't know. Despite this I cheer like a fool with my arms in the air celebrating when someone does something well. I give thumbs up liberally when it is warranted. I often stop swimmers in the middle of a 25 or 50 just to tell them that they're doing something well. We may move the goal posts on our swimmers, but by celebrating their achievements at each stage and giving positive feedback the swimmers look forward to mastering the next skill.

We run into problems with our swimmers when our goal, when our skill that we are doing, well exceeds the ability of our swimmers. If for example we were trying to work on side breathing, and our swimmers had no understanding of how to move the freestyle arms they would never be able to accomplish what our goal is.

I have a new swimmer that just started in the middle of summer. She came from swim lessons and is familiar with side glide and breathing on her back while she doggy paddles with one hand. Every time she needs to take a breath during a 25 freestyle she extends one arm, lays on her side or back, and begins paddling with the arm that was supposed to be doing a stroke. She takes two or three breaths while panting and puts her face back in the water to continue swimming until she runs out of air. If I were to introduce bilateral breathing, or both sides, it would be too far of a stretch for her to accomplish. Instead, I should focus on how to do a quick breath, or how to keep her arms moving while she takes a breath and put her face back in the water. For her stretching is learning how to take a breath without panting or taking multiple breaths while rotating onto her side or back.

Unfortunately this topic is so diverse and broad that I can't cover every swimming skill and provide the exact thing to stretch towards. Instead you need to discover for yourself what the next logical incremental progressive step is for your swimmer in what particular stage of swimming they are in.

When you choose what skills to do, or what activities you should do during your swim practices considered the average or baseline skill level of your group. If you're working with swimmers that don't know how to swim breaststroke it would be inappropriate for you to give them an activity where they have to do a breaststroke arm with the breath followed by the kick. Instead break up that skill into its component pieces and introduce them one at a time. Likewise if you have a group comprised of age group swimmers that are used to doing complicated sets using a clock don't give them a set in which they also need to keep track of their heart rate and stroke count. If your swimmers are not used to doing all those things as habits then it may be overwhelming for them to do all at once. Spend time tracking heart rate without an interval. Have them count their strokes during a simple interval set like on a minute or two minutes. Remove as many complicated mental barriers to attention as possible.

Layer in your new abilities slowly and with deliberate care.

We learn by expanding our experience, by attempting things that we cannot succeed at and failing. Stretching is the act of reaching beyond your comfort area and moving into territory with which you have little or no experience.

I think of myself as a guide. I know the path through the jungle to get to the summit and see the awesome waterfall. I can point out the missteps along the way, and teach my participants how to walk up the mountain without getting bitten by a snake or trapped in a landslide.

I wouldn't take my imaginary group of jungle mountain climbers directly to the impossible to scale slick cliff. I would take them along the well worn trail and teach them the skills they need along the way.

I expect most of my swimmers to initially fail at every new activity we introduce. The first time we do streamline with 11, E, 11 most swimmers rush through the sequence of moves or do them in the wrong order. We are introducing something new and different and failure is expected. If you read through the rest of this book you will know that we provide multiple avenues of feedback using targeted language to improve performance. Like the guy helping climbers we are coaching our swimmers as they stretch for the next level of ability through our instruction, our choice of activity, and our truthful acknowledgment of the success or failure.

Provide opportunities for your swimmers to stretch beyond their ability. Give them skills and activities that are familiar yet slightly different enough to stimulate their attention and imagination. Consider the next incremental step of whatever skill you are working on and offer that as a target or challenge.

Brain Food: keeping the appetite interested

———

We are drawn to the new and the different. Our brains are constantly on the hunt for stimulation and excitement. We like the floods of dopamine that flood our minds with joy and pleasure. Doing something you are good at or familiar with Ken sometimes produce those rush of hormones. We can also encourage interest and deliberate practice by providing challenges and activities that are interesting and just difficult enough to motivate the attention of our participants.

I spent a lot of time in this book talking about routines and habits. We review frameworks to use for all of your different skill acquisition activities but is that interesting enough to keep your participants excited about coming to practice?

I remember in the early days of my coaching having one parent constantly tell me that we were always doing the same thing every day. I knew, of course, that we weren't but that our framework was the same. I did learn from that parent that not everybody sees the same thing that I do. We needed to provide enough diversity and stimulation in our practices so that the kids weren't going home telling their parents that we always did the same thing.

Yes, we did the same warm-up and spent the first half of practice working on targeted skill acquisition using the 3X SL format. The second half of practice I started changing it up playing different games and activities, as well as coming up with different sets.

Our framework, and our habit adhering to routine makes learning new and challenging skills easier. We also have to provide games and diverse activities that provide both an interesting format and a reliance on the familiar to accomplish general goals.

Take for example our recent game, "save the coaches." In this game we draw out a map or a series of activities that correspond to a journey or a "quest." One recent quest was spelunking in the deep dark cave. I drew two swimmers standing in front of a big cave opening and mapped out four different areas that swimmers would need to go through in order to get a pouch of gold at the bottom of the cave. We did different drills and 25s, as well as dives off the blocks and streamlines. At each location there was a story that went with what they were doing. The first step of their journey was to swim underneath the large and sharp stalactites that hung from the ceiling to close to the surface of the water. Swimmers needed to streamline on their back underwater so as to not get caught up by the sharp edges. If they succeeded they came through unscathed, but if they got to the surface before a certain point they would get scratched and began bleeding.

The next stage of the spelunking was to travel through a large lake with a large open area. In this area were a horde of vampire bats and if they were cut up from their failure to streamline underwater on their back they were attacked by the bats. In order to remain human they needed to swat the bats away with their hands while doing backstroke kick for 50 yards. It's actually a drill that the Olympian Elizabeth Beisel described as "Titanic" where are you kick on your back with streamline arms perpendicular to the surface. This is a variation on that drill. It requires significant effort to keep above water while flailing your arms in the air.

If swimmers were unable to swat the bats away they were bitten by the vampire bats and Wood later turn into a vampire. In the end if they were vampires they would have to trade the gold for a potion that would turn them human again.

This game is a relatively new activity I've been doing with smaller groups in the summer. It highlights this very point I'm talking about in this chapter, keeping things interesting and feeding the brain in order to motivate our swimmers.

You may not have the luxury of coming up with a story and using a whiteboard to the same effect that I'm describing here. What I like about this game is that it provides something beyond inherent ability improvement to our swimmers efforts. These seven, eight, nine-year-olds that are participating in this activity are excited about the different and new quest that I've been coming up with. Yes they want to accomplish and achieve that goal stated in the quest, but they also have to demonstrate quality swimming skills in order to successfully progress through the quest line.

There are multiple and different ways that you can accomplish the same goal. Think about your group how you can provide something new and different yet still retain the same reliance on habit and routine in your swim practices.

Leverage those things that you always do. When we do 25s we organize ourselves in a certain manner on the wall and along the lane line. I call that "setting up your lane." That is a shortcut that we can rely on later on when we are swimming 25s in a set.

What things like that have you created you wouldn't have to worry about when coming up with a new or interesting game?

I feel like we can do these games with interesting and sometimes chaotic stories because my swimmers have a habit of getting out of the water and looking at the whiteboard while I explain our next portion of that practice.

I feel like I've built up habits over time with enough repetition and consistency that they fall into the framework easily enough that I'm not managing their behavior or where they should stand or what they should do. We can do these creative things because they rest on the frame work for which we've created and used.

I encourage you to experiment. I encourage you to come up with activities and have them fail. Make adjustments in the middle of them. Scrap them if they are not working the way you hoped. Come back the next day and iterate on your idea.

As of writing this chapter we have played the "save the coaches" quest about six times each with different results and each getting better and better, with less and less downtime in between. The more we play I find I'm better able to come up with new and interesting swimming related activities. The swimmers show genuine interest to improve their form and technique on certain pain points with which they failed on the previous quest.

I have swimmers that were not able to streamline on their back underwater now doing it for the required distance, to the flags. I feel like the failure within the "quests" to streamline underwater on their back and the associated consequences motivated them to improve their technique.

Your challenge is to balance your practices with familiar and old routines and habits, or frameworks, with new and interesting activities, skills, or ways of approaching swimming that will stimulate and excite your swimmer's minds.

I admit that many of the games I played during swim practices are a result of my own bordem. There are times that I'm bored of the routine and habit, and find myself annoyed with the regular format of warmup, two groups with deliberate practice and a longer set. There are times in the season when we need to reset or teach this format, and it works for a couple of months, but when I've had swimmers with me for a year or two and they're familiar with both the activities and general format I like to spice practice and their interest by doing diverse and different games.

Summer is an excellent time to experiment. Many of our swimmers participate in camps or swim lessons during the day and come to practice in the evening. I found that the strict appearance to lap swimming with intervals and boring drills tends to exhaust my swimmers both mentally and physically after a long day in the sun. For our developmental in beginning groups I generally play games or activities that are directly related to specific swimming skills but are presented in a interesting and amusing manner, generally offering significant opportunity for self improvement and choice.

At the beginning of every practice during the summer we have access to deep water and starting blocks. I let the swimmers do as many jobs or dives off the blocks as they please for the five minutes before practice officially starts. I've seen seven-year-olds who were terrified of the starting blocks now demand that we get a chance to leap off of them. I've seen other swimmers grow significantly in their streamlined ability even asking coaches for feedback as they practice on their own how to improve. This time is generally supervised but without direct coaching or instruction. My only requirements are that they do "some" dives. I would call it unstructured free time with a specific boundary; jumps or dives.

I feel like it is different enough for the swimmers to engage their interest, and motivate them to do things that they find amusing and fun. It also serves as a good transition between the playful amusement they are used to during the day at camp or at home on their own without school.

They know that when practice begins we immediately start with a 100 IM kick and easily slip into their lanes to begin our structured practice time.

In order to keep our swimmers minds interested, to whet their appetite with the new and stimulating, we iterate or make small changes to the formats we've done in the past.

The quest game is not really anything drastically different from anything else we do. The activities and challenges within the quest are all things that we've done in the past; three times streamlined on the surface, 2x25's position11, front flips, jumps off the blocks with a specific height requirement or distance. The story that goes around each of those activities and my interaction with the swimmers based on their performance is the difference. In itself it isn't anything drastically unique yet it is strange enough and the narrative I provide is an extreme deviation from the typical you do this, next to this mentality that we easily slip into as coaches.

I want you to take away from the section that you have a wide range of creative opportunity. Remember that we are working with children, we are working with kids whose imagination is as vibrant and diverse as any we can comprehend. I would argue that children's imagination is even more close to reality as they can walk inside of that fake world you create and live and breathe the net if you share that vision two. I certainly remember when I was younger feeling like my little country I created with small toys and miniature vehicles was just as real as the United States. What can you do during practice to excite your swimmers imagination? What can you do to tie in a swimming activity or skill even tenuously to something the kids can relate to or live in their imagination?

Our brains crave different and new. We rely on habit, routine, and the familiar but our motivated and interested by the new and challenging.

Doing It On The Fly

Remember the story I told you at the beginning of this book? The story about the developmental coach that didn't know what he was doing and would wander through practice with long speeches that went nowhere and had the kids waiting at the wall for 15 to 20 minutes without doing anything?

I'm grateful for experiencing those practices because they taught me what not to do. One of my crucial teaching tactics is to provide an opportunity to swimmers doing something wrong so they know what it feels like.

Do three streamlines where you do something incorrect. For example, do a streamline without locking your thumb. Do another streamline without squeezing your ears. This is one of those small activities that encourages our swimmers to do a skill incorrectly. By highlighting this wrong behavior we are in effect reinforcing the positive swimming skill by making our swimmers think about what is wrong. When they identify the incorrect behavior they are more likely to remember that in the future and if they catch themselves doing it self correct.

I often write developmental practices on the fly, or on the pool deck in the moment. I feel like I can do this because I have a long history of experience working with these ability groups and am able to draw on a diverse bank of skills and activities. My swimmers are familiar with our format and routine, and I can lean on that framework to swap in different skills and abilities with minor variations without disrupting the overall flow of our practices.

I found that one of the most challenging things for my assistant coaches to do is write a practice in the moment that is both fun and effective.

I imagine that it is a source of anxiety for my assistant coaches when they do something, or make a choice about how they are going to run practice. They have me watching their behavior and they have the kids looking at them for direction. My goal for training new assistant coaches is to treat them in a similar manner that I treat the swimmers. I want them to become familiar with failure and expect to get feedback based on how they can improve their coaching.

One of the first mistakes assistant coaches make is not having a specific targeting skill that they want to work on. They will often jump from butterfly to breaststroke, freestyle to backstroke, moving through a diverse set of skills in order to hit everything instead of aiming at one particular ability with multiple activities.

Most of my practices have a particular skill theme. For example we might be working on side breathing for freestyle. In order to reach that goal we will do different activities that approach it sideways. We might do three times streamline +5 kicks in position11 plus position one with one breath to the side and five more kicks with your face down. We would follow that with three times streamline five strokes of freestyle with one breath and a flip. I like doing a short aerobic set to either provide opportunity to practice what we've done in our small groups or to reset their brains so they can aim their attention at the specific skill. That might mean doing a 50 freestyle kick with friends or a 50 backstroke. It may not directly relate to side breathing, but it provides enough of a exhaustive aerobic swim or opportunity to do without thinking so that when we returned to our highly intensive deliberate practice the swimmers have the mental energy to aim their attention at what I'm asking them to.

Beginning assistant coaches often write practices on the fly without considering these details.

Another significant error I see with writing practices on the fly is doing something unique or different without clearly establishing the format or framework that that activity will use.

I highly suggest that if you are doing something drastically different from your normal routine or framework that you should build up to it slowly with small incremental introduction or miniature versions of that skill or activity.

The first time we play the game "true or false" we do only three questions. The rules are fairly simple, if I say something true jump in and if I say something false do not. If you get the answer wrong you are out as our swimmers participate in this game multiple times we can do more challenging questions and spend more time doing it because they are familiar with the routine that goes into playing the game.

This is a very simple example. If you're going to do something more complicated like a set with 20x25's where swimmers do something on the odds and something else on the evens you would want to introduce this concept multiple times with shorter sets so that your swimmers are gradually introduced to this concept.

Another example would be changing what the swimmer does within a 25. I often teach butterfly by doing a set of 25's where swimmers due to the four strokes of butterfly immediately after the streamline and then switch to freestyle for the rest the 25. We do the same thing for breaststroke, mainly to remove the anxiety about going fast for kids with an ineffective breast-stroke kick. Once swimmers get familiar with doing a certain number of strokes and then switching something else we can begin chaining together different strokes or things during our small group activities. We can do activities like three times streamline +1 fly +1 breaststroke. We can also start introduc-ing things like swim freestyle to halfway and backstroke kick the other half.

My point here is that if you're going to do something new and different make sure you have established something similar to it in the past or take deliberate steps during your practice to lead up to the more complicated set or activity. If you are go-ing to introduce something new and different from your nor-mal framework spent significant amount of time explaining it or breaking it into pieces with demonstrations so people know what to do. Ask yourself, "is this worth spending this amount of time explaining?"

Here are a few examples of what **not** to do:

• Speak for longer than three minutes. If your instructions are too complicated to explain in less than three minutes then you should not be doing that activity on the fly. Stick with the simple remain with the familiar and make only small iterative changes to your activities. Rely on what your swimmers already know when you're coming up with the practice without planning it in advance.

• Give swimmers a complex, complicated, multi step ability that they've never done before. Avoid doing something that is so mentally overwhelming that your swimmers need to memorize the activity and the series of steps that are doing. Most will do it wrong, others will struggle through a few transitions, and overall you will have a poorly executed swim.

• Do lots of short swimming skills that are unrelated. It is easy to think that coaching is telling swimmers what to do in a series of sequences. Most coaches that coach on the fly do things like 2x25 freestyle, 2x25s breaststroke, 2x25's fly, hundred freestyle kick, 100 breaststroke kick, and two dives. For developmental or teaching purposes this does nothing for our swimmers. It is a series of tasks designed only to eat up time and with such short distances and diverse skills does not provide an opportunity for the coaches to give feedback and see improvement in any one particular area.

• Use language or terminology that your swimmers are unfamiliar with without example or definition. If you say something and see blank stares, then define your terms. If you call streamline "rocketships" then give a visual example of what you are referring to. Coaches do not use the same terms for the same activities, even in the same club. Assume that your swimmers have no idea what you're talking about unless you've already defined your terms.

• Speak without certainty. I've seen veteran swim instructors tasked with coming up with an activity on the spot stumble through an activity with lots of "umms" "ahhhs," and long pauses while they think. Kids do not like casual and poorly thought out tasks. They'll resent the activity. They want you to be in control and they want the coaches to present a confident and knowledgeable demeanor. If you're speaking like, "We're going to do... uhmmmm 2 x 25's... no! 2 x 50's of uhmmmm, ahhh, freestyle with uhm, Breaststroke arms," they're going to feel like you're just coming up with something for them to do to kill time without a purpose. They're going to be asking themselves, "why are we doing this?" We want our swimmers to feel empowered by our tasks and our activities, like everything we do is aiming to some specific purpose of improvement. I tell my swimmers frequently; everything we do has a purpose. The more curious ones find that connection or ask about it, and the others that don't care or aren't interested get the benefit of the connection without knowing exactly why.

• Persist in something that does not work. Avoid doubling down on a bad activity. Just like your swimmers won't do everything perfectly the first time neither will you. You will fail when you come up with a new activity on the fly. You are going to create new activities that are ineffective and are more grueling and task oriented than they are fun. I have often cut connectivity short apologizing for the mistake and moving on to something else. If you find that you are spending too much time explaining things or that your swimmers do not understand exactly what they should be doing and stop reexplain your instructions or move on to something else. Doubling down on a poor game or a bad activity frustrates both the coaches and swimmers. Knowing when to admit your failure and learn from that mistake is a crucial step an example of a veteran teacher.

I have one suggestion that will make your practices that you write on the fly better. Write down or save a large bank of skills and activities that you do regularly. I used to write all of my practices in travel.com, but with recent changes have moved all of my practices and activities to www.swimminglessonsideas.com. Using reusable blocks I've created a bank of skills categorized by stroke and format which I can pull from when I write a practice. Having written everything down and drawn out examples and pictures for each activity I have a large bank of things to do in my memory. (You can see my daily practices when you subscribe to the Developmental Swim Practices at https://swimminglessonsideas.com/store/ . It includes pictures, games, guides, and progressions)

I encourage you to do something similar. Write down all of the things you ever do during practice and organize them in some fashion so that you can easily look through them off the pool deck. The more familiar you are with all the different things you do at practice the easier it will be to draw from that bank of knowledge when you are attempting to write a practice on the fly.

I think the best thing about writing practices on the fly is that you can tailor the activities and skill work to whoever is at practice on that day. I recommend that you follow a general season plan in which you are introducing broad concepts in a structured pace ensuring that you get exposure to every stroke across a season, but on a day-to-day basis you can highlight specific skill work tailored to who has shown up for practice on that particular day.

I often make small changes to practices that I've written in advance because I want to reinforce specific skills based on who came to practice that evening. For example, if I have a heavy contingent of swimmers that need work on breaststroke kick, and I've written a practice that is more focused on breaststroke arms and breathing I might adjust the progression of skills to accommodate the needs of those breaststroke kicking participants.

I draw from my skill bank and memory to swap and activities that align with the format and framework.

Think about practices that were disaster for you. Have you seen Coach run a terribly ineffective practice? What did they do?

What are some signs of your swimmers being so bored that they stopped listening?

Making a mental note or writing down examples in which you have seen an effective coaching will help you avoid those mistakes in the future.

Writing and running practices on the fly provides a interesting and stimulating specifically tailored environment but comes with significant pitfalls if you are not prepared. Lean on your previous framework, speak clearly and directly, keep your instruction short and brief, and work through a progression of skills. Follow the steps and you will have fun and effective impromptu swim practices.

Final Thoughts

———

You can create fun and effective developmental swim practices. You can.

I believe there is a process to commanding a group of swimmers that you can learn in a few short steps.

1. Know your material. Have a good idea of what skills you need to work towards and break those skills into small progressive steps. Know the nuance of streamline, of freestyle breathing to the side and think about how you can get someone to do what you want by succeeding at smaller achievable steps. A 25 of full freestyle with side breathing is difficult. How can you chunk that skill into smaller pieces, teach those parts then put it all back together?

2. Rely on a framework to organize your participants, run your activities, and provide clear expectations. Routines are good. Make the details different to provide stimulation, interest, and excitement at doing something new.

3. Leverage your framework to play games that appeal to imagination, and provide challenge. Overcoming difficulty is rewarding. Children like to have a task that they cannot accomplish. Set the goal just beyond their easily achievable ability. Provide stretching opportunities.

As I finish this book I'm in the last weeks of summer and I'm looking at Fall. Many of the swimmers in my Developmental 2 group want to move into the first Age Group group in our program. To do that they need to do a 25 of each stroke legally. Breaststroke and Fly are difficult to teach and even harder for children to succeed at.

We've spent the last few weeks of summer in the 50 meter pool when we've been at a 25 pool the entire rest of the year. Because it is the end of the year we tend to play games in the diving well for half of practice. My challenge has been to still provide instruction while giving opportunity to have fun. Using the methods I've outlined in this book my practices at the 50 meter pool have been this:

100 IM Kick

2 x 50's 1/2 Position 11, 1/2 Free swim.

Get out of the water. Talk about next set.

4 x 50's. Swim Fly to the first yellow, then backstroke or freestyle the rest of the 50, swimmer's choice. The fly is a "test" for the next group. Demonstrate that you can do all four portions legally and you'll pass the "test."

I follow up with every swimmer and give them specific feedback if they got disqualified for an illegal stroke and how they can improve. At this point in the season they should know all of the components of the strokes. They should know how to do each portion, or at least be aware of them. People on the verge who simply need to focus their attention on the skill will aim it, and those that are unable will at least stretch for what they are capable of.

We can't do this type of dangling carrot all of the time, but for the last few weeks of the season it works wonders.

5-10 minutes of games in the diving well. We have about 20 swimmers, so we line them up along one side, and give them a series of challenges.

Challenge 1:Streamline with only streamline from one side to the other. If you fall out of streamline you're out, if you touch anyone you're both out.

Challenge 2: Streamline with one flip before you get to the wall. Same rules about getting out.

Challenge 3: Do 3 strokes of Breaststroke without touching anyone else, same rules as above.

Challenge 4: Kick on back in airplane. Same rules.

Challenge 5: Kick on back goggles off, eyes closed. If you open your eyes or go on belly you're out, and same other rules.

4 x 50's swim BR to the first yellow, then backstroke or freestyle the rest of the 50. Swimmer's choice. The breaststroke is a "test" for the next group. Demonstrate that you can do all four portions legally and you'll pass the "test."

More games in the diving well.

Every day I attempt to provide a stimulating and interesting environment for the swimmers to excel in. I want to give them opportunity to succeed, but also have fun. I think that some of joy my participants feel is from the air and atmosphere of respect. I do my best not to belittle my swimmers, not to bark orders and shout with anger in my voice. There are times when I'm upset and I've said things that I shouldn't have, but I do my best to remember that I'm working with children, and unless they're doing something that might cause someone harm, the stakes are very low. They're at a sport, at an activity, they're at practice to learn, to improve, and above all for them: to have fun.

How do you provide a fun and interesting environment for swimmers to demonstrate the swimming skills you've taught?

How do you encourage deliberate practice?

How do you allow swimmers to approach difficulty and failure?

I tell swimmers, children, that they failed an attempt. We even use a thumbs down and say the word, "fail."

When they succeed though, I shout "Success!" and give a thumbs up.

Do you have a culture where failure, where not meeting the objective is expected, allowed, and safe?

You can run fun and effective swim practices. Through practice, through attention to your behavior, through providing an encouraging and stimulating environment you'll have engaged swimmers that want to succeed and will welcome the new challenges you put in their path.

If you have questions, want more information, or want to give me your perspective reach out:

Jeff@swimmingideas.com

Twitter: @swimmingideas

Instagram: @swimmingideas

TLDR: too long didn't read

———

Setup a framework that you do every day. Make it a "system" or a format that you can swap out different activities while following the same track. Make activities a 'little' difficult for the people doing them. Play games that have a purpose. Have fun, praise effort, and avoid being a punitive yelling jerk.

Made in the USA
Coppell, TX
20 December 2019

13564174R00066